Six Biblical Issues Against "God Is In Control"

Larry Adams

Other Books By Larry Adams

Discipling A New Believer
Revelation: A Fresh Perspective
Out On A Limb
That Your Prayers May Not Be Hindered
Did You Ever Realize...
Future Focus

Psalms 25:12-13 (NASB) "*12 Who is the man who fears the Lord? He will instruct him in the way he should choose.13 His soul will abide in prosperity, And his descendants will inherit the land.*"

Contents

Basic Concepts

Many people believe that God is in control.

Nowhere in Scripture does it actually state "God is in control." That statement also requires that the original language backs up the translation. A case in point to illustrate this is, 2 Corinthians 5:14. This verse starts out with, "*The love of God controls us...*" In the Greek, the word translated "controls" really means "to hold together." So that verse is really saying that the love of God holds us together. There is no concept of "control" involved in that verse. This ties in with the statement Jesus made that they will know we are his disciples because of our love for one another. (John 13:35)

In my searching the scriptures, I first looked for those exact four words "God is in control," but could not find that. I searched for synonyms of control that are related to the word "God" or "Lord" in verses in the Bible. What I looked for was a phrase that would very obviously mean the same thing as those four specific words. By "very obvious" what I mean is, if someone wanted to confuse that statement to make it look like it did not mean God is in control, they would have to go through extreme gyrations of word redefinition and grammar changes in order to make it look other than what it obviously means. I still could not find anything in scripture that identifies clearly in words: "God is in control."

I also looked at this situation from another angle. I read the approximately 478 instances of the word "love" in the NASB. In all the descriptions of love, and all the applications of love, nothing indicated any kind of "control" of, or over, the one being loved. If God is love, along with his righteousness, justice, etc., his love is devoid of any kind of "control," then it should be obvious that those he loves, he

1

does not control. Please be careful not to confuse control over what we call "forces of nature" (wind, waves, etc.) and control over demons, with control over people, those created in his image and likeness.

Primary Distinction:

God _can_ control what most people would call "forces of nature" - wind, seas, weather, earthquakes, bad viruses, bad bacteria, physical deformities - and demons, things that are not made in His image and likeness, usually by direct verbal command at the moment of need. Just because God can control these things, does not mean that God _must always_ be in constant, unrelenting, poking, prodding, pulling, pushing, tweaking, control of every breath, quiver, etc., otherwise these things would not function at all. God does not control those made IN His image and likeness, i.e. people, in the same manner as forces of nature and demons. This will be the focus of discussion. This does not mean anything even close to God does not control anything, His word makes a clear distinction between forces of nature and demons versus people, those made in His image and likeness.

Too many times we refer to a situation as Satan has labeled it, and that masks what is the real, underlying issue. This issue needs to be clarified. God can control demons and forces of nature. God is not the grand puppet-master constantly tweaking the puppet strings of those two categories. As His purpose and need comes about, He can intervene into the affairs of the world and exercise control over those two categories. The following Issues from the Scriptures demonstrate that when it comes to those created in His own image and likeness, that He does not control people, He does not exercise power over people to cause something in anything similar to the farmer in the pre-1800's who had to have both hands on the plow and the reins to the ox or horses and was constantly yelling, pulling, pushing, twisting, just to get a furrow plowed. God was not stupid when He created the universe, earth, and all that is in them. God created animals, planets, weather, etc., and people to "function" in certain ways. God then "turned on the switch" and those created things started functioning as God had created them. God is still sovereign over all simply because things function as He created them to function Some people, particularly those back in the years before mechanical and computer automation, have a very difficult time mentally understanding that things, including people, can function as designed and do not require the creator to be constantly manipulating and prodding those creations in each and every movement and thought and belief and action possible. How many hands and fingers would God require in order to constantly keep tweaking all the puppet strings of every thing and person so that He is in constant control of everything? He would make the Hindu god Vishnu look like a childish amateur.

If I create a computer game where there are characters the player can assign attributes, skills, and capabilities, and whatever those may be, can work together to evaluate the environment and randomly make choices of action in that environment, and those characters work as I have designed them, then I am still sovereign over that game and characters, even though my human mental abilities may not be able to contrive what all the possible outcomes may be. I am still sovereign over that game, in spite of my human limitations, simply because the game and characters function the way I designed them to function. We dare not take our own human limitations and impose them onto God. We are the ones who are limited, not God. The capabilities we have from God give us a small clue to who God is and what He is like, but He is always greater than His creation. God can always do more, and do it better, than anything we could possibly imagine.

And that always includes foreknowing what the result is for any "random" situation we may find ourselves in.

Romans 2:11 (NASB) "*11 For there is no partiality with God.*"

James 1:17b (NASB) "*17...the Father of lights, with whom there is no variation or shifting shadow.*"

James 2:9 (NASB) "*9 But if you show partiality, you are committing sin and are convicted by the law as transgressors.*"

These three verses identify that God does not show partiality (or favoritism) and that showing partiality is sin. So, those who think that God's only attribute is "Sovereignty" are declaring that God is sinning by showing partiality to only one of His characteristics. If there is one significant characteristic of God identified in the Scripture, it is love, but that does not override any of the other of his characteristics. All God's characteristics are "balanced," not skewed in favor of one over the others. God's law is identified on the basis of love, but His law also includes justice, and punishment for sin – balance...

Romans 8:29 (NASB) begins: "*29 For those whom He foreknew, He also predestined to become conformed to the image of His Son,...*" Some religious groups substitute "foreordained" in place of "foreknew." And then they build their philosophy on their own substituted word. That obviously is a mutilation of Scripture since "foreknew" does not mean the same thing as "foreordained." Their problem is that in human terms, we cannot know the future, meaning we cannot "foreknow" anything unless we declare that thing as a goal of some sort and work to achieve it. God is not limited like people. God can foreknow everything in His creation. He knows the end from the beginning (Isa. 46:10). Many translations use a word like "declares" in Isa 46:10, and commentators treat the word as though it meant "decrees" or "commands" when the word really means: (CWSB Dictionary) "H5046. נָגַד nāgaḏ: A verb meaning to tell, to report, to make known, to explain, to be reported." This word has no connotations of demand, command, decree, or anything like that. To "declare" something has only to do with telling or making known, like the early 1900's when newsboys would sell newspapers on the street corner, yelling out the headlines. – the newsboys did not create the headlines, they only tell about it. Here again we see theologians taking human limitations and imposing them onto God. Some religious philosophies are simply a glorification of human limitations that have nothing Godly about them.

Logical Consequence

Logical consequence is something that those who twist the Scriptures hate worse than all the plagues and disasters in world history combined. Logical consequence is when someone starts with a statement of condition or situation, and the logical consequences of that statement are followed. Sometimes this is referred to as following something to its logical conclusion These consequences are followed until there are no more steps possible. At that point the steps produce something that is still logical and sensible and provable, or a step is reached that is obviously illogical, highly improbable, or downright contradictory to proven fact, or obviously contradictory to the initial statement or condition. If the end step is sensible and logical, that means the initial statement started from is also sensible and logical, i.e. true. If the last step is illogical or contradictory to other characteristics of the initial statement, then the initial statement started from is also illogical, i.e. not true.

Logical consequence can be an important part of understanding God's word. God is not a God of chaos (1 Cor. 14:33), God is orderly and sensible. Sometimes we fail to see the immediate sensibility of something, but God sees into the future where we cannot see and understands the greatest good that can be. We say that hindsight is 20-20, and sometimes we do need to wait and we will also understand. However, when we reach logical consequences that mean something like "God is love at the same time that God is hate," or "God is holy and righteous, and at the same time God is evil," there is something inherently wrong with those contrasts, and the initial starting statement is obviously wrong. Some do not think that logic can be used to understand the bible. Those whom I have discussed this with have consistently used logic to attempt to prove that logic cannot be used to understand the bible – rather hypocritical of them. Logical consequence will be used within this article even if it makes you think harder than you usually prefer.

Category Errors:

This situation happens more frequently than most people would think. Let me illustrate this situation with an example. I have talked to unbelievers about spiritual warfare, simplistically, the idea of good versus evil. Some have retorted that demons do not exist today because of our advanced society and technology. I have demonstrated that in the Old Testament there are records of people behaving then, several thousand years ago, that match up perfectly with situations in our modern society. That simply means people have not changed. Then, regarding demons don't exist because of our modern technology, I simply ask then what physical technology has to do with spiritual demons. It never occurred to them that they were committing a category error by equivocating something physical with something spiritual when they really have totally different environments and characteristics. Physical technology has nothing to do with anything spiritual. That is an example of a category error, mixing things togeth-

6

er as though they related to each other when in reality they have nothing to do with each other.

God relates to people on the basis of persuasion through His voice, not any kind of programmed control, force, or coercion. (See Issue 1) Over 20 times Paul used a form of the word "persuade" to describe the intent and process behind his preaching the Gospel to both Jew and Gentile. God approaches us with the Gospel in a persuasive manner, and when we believe on Jesus, the Holy Spirit continues to persuade us to do those things which have been commanded, and those things which are pleasing to God (God's will). God does not change, He uses the right "tool" for the job. The word translated "will" is from a Greek word which means:

"(CWSB Dictionary) *"2307. θέλημα thélēma; gen. thelḗmatos, neut. noun from thélō (G2309), to will. The suffix -ma indicates that it is the result of the will. Will, not to be conceived as a demand, but as an expression or inclination of pleasure towards that which is liked, that which pleases and creates joy. When it denotes God's will, it signifies His gracious disposition toward something."*

Note that "will" is not to be conceived as a demand. Many people have a difficult time with this because theologians over the centuries have made a category error in mixing "will" and "command," when "will" has no concept of demand as a "command" would. In just about every Systematic Theology book I've read, God's will has been a subset of God's decrees and commands. I'm just stunned that these theologians seem to have never looked up the meaning of the word in the Greek.

1 Peter 2:1 (NASB) *"¹ But false prophets also arose among the people, just as there will also be false teachers among you, who will secretly introduce destructive heresies, even denying the Master who bought them, bringing swift*

7

destruction upon themselves."

Peter warned us that false teachers would arise from among the disciples, and this category error with the words "will" and "command" is a good example of that. God's will is simply that which pleases or makes Him joyful – it is not a command. When we determine God's will in a situation or for our life, we treat it like a command instead of something that would make Him happy (something indicative of a real relationship, like child to parent). Of course, and obviously, obeying His commands makes him happy with us, but, if you carefully study the things God commands, they all relate to three categories, our relation to God, our relation to each other, and what I call "Personal Reflection," how we handle our own thoughts, emotions, attitudes, etc. See my book "Discipling A New Believer by Larry Adams" for a much more complete dissertation on Jesus commands to His disciples. We will touch on this particular issue of "will" versus "command" near the end of the book.

As you read the following Issues, please be careful to understand that this discussion has nothing to do with any idea like "God doesn't control anything." God can control things, but the Scriptures clearly identify there is a difference between "forces of nature" and demons versus people. The satanic label of "God is in control" masks and confuses the real point as identified in Scripture. Just because God can control something, does not require that He be in constant, unrelenting manipulation of everything so that something can happen.

*There is one possible "exception" to God does not control people – the ministry/gift of prophet. The caveat that goes along with this is that the ministry is designed to speak a specific word from God to a specifitd group of people. God does command the prophet for what is to be said, how it is to be said and to whom it isto be said. Other than that specific instance, God does not make any other commands of his prophets other than what He has given in His Law, and the over 70 commands given by Jesus which all are regarding relationships, how they are to be handled or managed.

Issue 1: Oppression is from the devil

Acts 10:38 (NASB) *"[38] You know of Jesus of Nazareth, how God anointed Him with the Holy Spirit and with power, and how He went about doing good and healing all who were oppressed by the devil, for God was with Him."*

Oppression means *"to exercise power over another."* In the context of Acts 10, it is obvious that the focus of this devilish oppression is people. Control means *"the power to cause someone or something to behave a certain way or believe a certain thing."* Oppression is the use of power to cause people to do things or believe things and they have no power to resist or refuse. (The power of Christ overcomes the Devil's oppression, people do not have that power in the flesh.) God does not use any form of power to cause us to behave a certain way or believe a certain thing, that would be oppression which is from the devil.

Matthew 20:25-28 is where Jesus describes the Gentile kings lording it over their people, but it is not that way among the disciples. Jesus then goes on to describe the greatest in the kingdom is the servant of all. (See also Mat. 20:28; Mk. 10:45; Jn. 13:1-17) Many people will read this passage and only identify the idea of the greatest in the kingdom is the servant of all and completely miss the point Jesus is making by contrasting the ways of Satan and the world versus the ways of the kingdom of God. The servant of all describes the relation between God and his children. God does *NOT* "lord it over" those who are his own, the opposite of the kings of the Gentiles. "Lord it over" is a simple figure of speech indicating control over another, or exercising power over another. God does not exercise control over His own, i.e. people, those made in His own image and likeness.

Jesus, in John 14:9, identifies that if you have seen Jesus, you have see the Father. In Matt. 20:28, Mark 10:45, Jesus identifies that He came to serve, not to be served (as the Gentile kings would require). God does not change, so, that means in the Kingdom of God (or heaven) that God is the greatest, and also the servant of all. The compete opposite of what takes place in the satanic, worldly, kingdoms of people here on Earth.

Mat. 12:24-32 and Mark 3:22-30 describe the Jewish leaders accusing Jesus of casting out demons by the power of Beelzebul (Beelzebub in NKJV), a nickname of Satan. Jesus gives a two pronged response, one about a house divided against itself cannot stand, and then a statement about blasphemy of the Son will be forgiven, but blasphemy of the Holy Spirit will not be forgiven. The accusation was calling the holy, righteous acts of Jesus an act of Satan. Some religious philosophies describe the new birth event as the Holy Spirit forcing (exercising power) salvation on people who cannot choose or desire it. Acts 10:38 identifies oppression, exercising power over a person, as being satanic. Therefore, these religious philosophies are taking a satanic action and applying it to the Holy Spirit. This is obviously blasphemy of the Holy Spirit. This using force over people is not the way God works.

Jonah is a good example of God not controlling people. As you read through the book of Johan, you will see that Jonah could hear God's voice, and chose to disobey. God used the weather to get the boat crew to throw him overboard. God used the fish to swallow Jonah and deliver him to the shore near Nineveh. After Nineveh repented, God raised up a plant to shade Jonah, and then used a worm to kill the plant. In none of these situations did God directly control Jonah. God controlled forces of nature, not oppression to achieve His goals in Jonah.

Let's take a look at another situation related to satanic oppression versus the way of God's kingdom. In the Old Testament, God told the Israelites that they were not to get involved in any manner with the false gods of the tribes currently living in the promised land (which were to be evicted by the Israelites). This starts in Exodus chapters 20 through 24. God warns them that those false gods will be a snare to them. A more detailed look at those false gods shows that they had a god for every physical need and fleshly desire, sex, food, children, money, power over people, etc. The pagan gods represent the exact opposite of what goes on in God's kingdom. The greatest in God's kingdom is God himself, who is the greatest servant of all. One of the most common names for those false gods was the "Baalim," or the "Baals." That word can be translated as either "master," or "owner." When the Israelites worshiped the Baals, the Baals became their master and owner. When the Israelites worshiped God at His Temple, the Israelites were free from the bondage and oppression of the false gods, and as Jesus stated, that burden is easy and light – the opposite of the oppression of the Baals. God's kingdom is the opposite of the ways of Satan and the world's oppressive system.

Issue 2: Love does not "control"

Love's definition/description and application, throughout both Old Testament and New Testament, contains nothing requiring nor implying control. If you love someone, there is no control of the one being loved, the one receiving the love. In the NASB, the word love is used about 478 times. I've taken the time to read each one in its context and have failed to find "control" as a part of love.

1 Corinthians 13:4-8a (NASB) *"⁴ Love is patient, love is kind and is not jealous; love does not brag and is not arrogant, ⁵ does not act unbecomingly; it does not seek its own, is not provoked, does not take into account a wrong suffered, ⁶ does not rejoice in unrighteousness, but rejoices with the truth; ⁷ bears all things, believes all things, hopes all things, endures all things. ⁸ Love never fails."*

(CWSB Dictionary) *"327. ἀναζητέω anazētéō; contracted anazētṓ, fut. anazētḗsō, from aná (G0303), an emphatic, and zētéō (G2212), to seek. To seek diligently."*

(Greek-English Lexicon, The - by Louw & Nida) *"27.42 ἀναζητέω (includes: ἐπιζητέω[a]) to try to learn the location of something by searching for it (presumably somewhat more emphatic or goal-directed than in the case of ζητέω a to try to learn where something is, 27.41) - to seek, to search, to try to find out by looking for."*

None of the listed characteristics of love indicate, either directly or by inference or implication, that love contains or uses any form of control. Not even the concept of "seek." See Genesis 3:8-10 where God called out to Adam, "Where are you?" God did not "seek" them, but, left it up to Adam and Eve to respond from their own initiative instead of "seeking" them out (Yes, God is all knowing, which is why He does not have to "seek," but, for us people, we don't know it all). Love desires a non-preprogrammed, non-forced response of

13

love. "Controlled Love," is not love at all, just a disguise for the oppression of the devil which can only be evil and hateful.

2 Corinthians 5:14 (NASB) *"14 For the love of Christ controls us, having concluded this, that one died for all, therefore all died,"*

The word "controls" in this verse turns out to be a bad translation. The word in the Greek means: "to hold together." This verse is really stating that "the love of Christ holds us together. This "holding" is from one believer to another. This goes along with Jesus statement:

John 13:35 (NASB) *"35 By this all men will know that you are My disciples, if you have love for one another."*

Again, there is no "control" involved within love in any form or manner.

1 John 4:7-10 (NASB) *"7 Beloved, let us love one another, for love is from God; and everyone who loves is born of God and knows God. 8 The one who does not love does not know God, for God is love. 9 By this the love of God was manifested in us, that God has sent His only begotten Son into the world so that we might live through Him. 10 In this is love, not that we loved God, but that He loved us and sent His Son to be the propitiation for our sins."*

God is love. If that is really true (and it really is...) then God does not control us, otherwise He could not be love. One of the significant points of 1 John 4:7-10 is that His love expresses itself to people, those created in His image and likeness, and not toward things that are not people. Jesus did not die on the cross to provide eternal life for rocks, or grass, or trees, or water, demons, or bad viruses, etc., only people.

Issue 3: We are created in God's image and likeness

Genesis 1:26 (NASB) *"[26] Then God said, "Let Us make man in Our image, according to Our likeness; and let them rule over the fish of the sea and over the birds of the sky and over the cattle and over all the earth, and over every creeping thing that creeps on the earth." "*

Mankind is created in God's image and likeness – if mankind is created as a controlled being, then also, God is a controlled being, and who controls God? This is such a ludicrous and illogical statement - that someone controls God - that the basic premises that lead to that conclusion must be in error. Therefore, mankind is not created as a controlled being. This is a good example of Logical Consequence proving that something in the basic premises is wrong.

Notice also that what was given to mankind to "control" is forces of nature...

Issue 4: "The Golden Rule"

Before we dig into the details on the Golden Rule, let's take a look at something few people ever pay attention to. Paul tells us that he would not have known that "coveting" is a sin unless the Law stated "You will not covet." (Rom. 7:7) The Law, primarily, but not limited to, the Ten Commandments, defines what is sin. The Law that God gave actually includes more than just the Ten Commandments. There were many other things that went along with the initial Ten. Many of the specific items within the Law also identify God's personality and character, and what it is for God to be holy. God does not sin, meaning at the least, God does not break the Ten Commandments; or any other of His Laws. The Golden Rule falls into this dual effect category of identifying what is sin and something about God's character and personality, His holiness.

Matthew 7:12 (NASB) *"12 "In everything, therefore, treat people the same way you want them to treat you, for this is the Law and the Prophets."*

Here, God's Law includes doing to others as you would have them do to you. By Jesus stating that "this is the Law and the Prophets," Jesus is stating that this "Golden Rule" is the sum and substance of the entirety of the Law. How inconsistent would it be for God to give us this Law, but He Himself behave in a different manner or opposite to what He requires of us? God is not a God of chaos. (1 Cor. 14:33) God gives us a detrimental view of being inconsistent, or double-minded, (Ps. 119:113; Jas. 1:8, 4:8) so why would anyone think that it is alright for God to have a double standard of behavior? (Double standard meaning, God behaving differently than what He wants of us. This double standard could also be stated as – it is not OK for us to sin, but if God does the same thing it is not sin for him) The truth of the
16

matter is that God treats/interacts with people in the same way that He wants us to treat/interact with Him. This interaction is based on a love response to what is pleasing to God (His "will"--meaning, wish, desire, intent, with no concept of demand). Jesus came to serve, not to be served, and we are to serve Him in like manner. Luke 6:31 is also a record of the Golden Rule

Matthew 22:37-40 (NASB) *"37 And He said to him, " 'You shall love the Lord your God with all your heart, and with all your soul, and with all your mind.' 38 This is the great and foremost commandment. 39 The second is like it, 'You shall love your neighbor as yourself.' 40 On these two commandments depend the whole Law and the Prophets."* "

In Matthew 7:12, Jesus states that this Golden Rule is the Law and the Prophets. In Matthew 22:37-40, Jesus states that loving God and your neighbor is what the whole Law and Prophets depend on. That very effectively makes the Golden Rule equivalent to the two greatest commandments. All the Law that God gave Moses at Mt. Sinai, is at least to teach us what we must do and how we must behave, and what we must not do – i.e. what is sin. God does not tell us to be holy and then Himself be unholy – He tells us to be holy because He is holy. (1 Peter 1:16; Lev 11:44f; 19:2; 20:7, 26; 21:8) God's nature is revealed in the Law He gave. God does not steal, murder, etc. God is Love according to John in his first letter. God expects us to love Him – He is loving us and expects us to love Him in return. It could be described as a vicious circle, God loves us, we love God, and round and round it goes.

If "God controls people," and He is treating us as He wants us to treat Him, then The Golden Rule requires that we control God in return. "We control God in return" is such a ludicrous, illogical statement that it should be obvious the basic premise of "God controls people" is wrong. (See Logical Consequence above)

This brings us to a question that must have an answer from the bible. The Holy Spirit persuades us to believe on Jesus for salvation, and thereafter, also persuades us to do those things that are pleasing to Him. God treats us with love and persuasion, not force, coercion, irresistible pre-programming, or anything like that (see Issue 1 above). "The Golden Rule" would then require us to treat God with love and persuasion. To most people, the idea of "persuading" God sounds very strange and foreign to their sense of "religiosity." Let's examine this further.

Exodus 32:9-10 (NASB) *"9 The Lord said to Moses, "I have seen this people, and behold, they are an obstinate people. 10 Now then let Me alone, that My anger may burn against them and that I may destroy them; and I will make of you a great nation.""*

This is a very serious indictment against the Israelites. Let's note some things about the context of this statement of God. This took place within an ongoing conversation between Moses and God that lasted about 40 days. This was not "out of the blue" as we say, it was not a standalone statement. Moses responded to this statement by persuading God to change his mind by identifying how the Egyptians would have a valid reason to "bad-mouth" God, and that it could be in violation of His promise to Abraham, Isaac, and Jacob (His unconditional covenant). God had very good reason to punish the Israelites, they were in violation of much of the Law that had already been identified to them.

There are many passages in the Old Testament that identify the fact that God does not change. We need to examine this carefully and not make unwarranted assumptions. God's penalty for sin is death (Rom. 6:23; Ezk. 18:20). However, a substitute for that required death can be presented on behalf of the sinner. That is what is behind the Old Testament sacrifice laws and what salvation in Jesus involves. God does not change in respect to the penalty required for sin, but is willing for another death to be substituted. This was eventually worked out for the Israelites and all mankind through Jesus.

Here in the dialog between Moses and God, we have Moses persuading God to "change His mind" in respect to the immediate punishment of the sins of Israel. Moses, without putting it into specific words, convinced God that there is a better way to handle this. God eventually let the present generation of Israelites who were disobedient, to die off naturally in the wilderness and let the following generation enter the promised land. Moses persuasion was a key part of this, and those rebellious ones still got the death they deserved.

We, similarly to Moses, can persuade God in some respects. Note again that this persuasion by Moses was part of an ongoing dialog with God. This was not a spastic outburst like Jephthah's ill-conceived bargaining with God which resulted in human sacrifice in Judges chapter 11 (also see below in Issue 6). Everything Moses brought up had to do with God's promises and holiness. We can take a similar position with God as Moses did, but, be careful that your persuasion stays in line with His Law (in light of the details and descriptions of His holiness) and all other aspects of God's personality and character. And just as importantly, we must be asking according to His will (what is pleasing to Him), and according to what is His purpose (Rom. 8:28), and on the basis of an on-going discussion/relationship with Him.

Issue 5: God put mankind in control of Earth to begin with.

Genesis 1:28 (NASB) "*28 God blessed them; and God said to them, "Be fruitful and multiply, and fill the earth, and subdue it; and rule over the fish of the sea and over the birds of the sky and over every living thing that moves on the earth."*"

(CWSB Dictionary) "*H3533.* כָּבַשׁ *kābaš: A verb meaning to subdue, to bring into subjection, to enslave. It means basically to overcome, to subdue someone. It is used to describe God's mandate to humans to subdue the created order (Gen. 1:28). It describes Israel's taking of the Promised Land, Canaan (Num. 32:22, 29; Josh. 18:1). King David subjugated the land (2 Sam. 8:11). It means to put into bondage or to degrade in general (Neh. 5:5). It is used once of Haman's supposed assault on Queen Esther (Esth. 7:8). It is used in its causative stem to indicate subduing or subjugating peoples (Jer. 34:11).*"

(MED) "*[3899]* כָּבַשׁ *kābaš 14x [Q] to subdue, overcome, enslave; [N] be subdued, be subject, be brought under control;*"

The word "control," meaning "the power to cause some one or thing to behave or believe something," fits very well with Genesis 1:28. God put mankind in control of Earth to begin with. This matches up with the discussion at the beginning of this book where I identified that God can control forces of nature and demons. Here God is delegating His control of the Earth to mankind, not control of people.

It seems extremely strange and absurd for God to give control of Earth to people and then control them in their controlling Earth while at the same time controlling everything on Earth. Why the middle man? God is not a God of chaos. Have you ever had a job, or known someone in their job, where the supervisor keeps interfering with what you are supposed to be doing – i.e. the supervisor is doing your job for you? The job never seems to get done well or maybe never seems to be done in time, or requires last minute reversals, etc. The job never goes well and usually results in a poor performance review. That is not God's way of doing things. God does not "control" people.

Issue 6: The instigator of a scheme is the one guilty of the results

First, the background principle illustrated. In 2 Samuel 12:1-15 we have recorded the incident of the prophet Nathan coming to King David to voice God's condemnation of David taking Bathsheba in adultery and having her husband Uriah killed in battle. David saw Bathsheba and sent for her to come to his palace and got her pregnant. David then devised a scheme to have her husband come home from battle and lie with his wife thereby "assuming" the fatherhood of Bathsheba's child – that failed miserably. David then devised a way for the Israelite army to leave Uriah stranded in battle where the enemy would kill him, thereby permitting David to marry Bathsheba, making the child look legitimate to the public. Uriah was killed in battle, and God sent Nathan to David. Nathan told David what amounted to a parable about a poor man who had a lamb that was part of the family. The lamb was stolen by a rich man who did not want to slaughter one of his own sheep in order to feed a visitor, but stole and killed the poor man's lamb. David was enraged and said the rich man must die and make restitution 4-fold. Nathan told David that he was that man, David had sinned against God.

The enemies at the battle were the ones who wielded a sword or spear to get Uriah killed, but God put the blame, sin and responsibility on David because he had instigated the scheme. God will eventually hold both David and the enemy at the battle guilty as in Isaiah 10:5-19 where He holds the Assyrians guilty even though they were used by God to punish Israel for their sins. God denied David building the temple later because God identified David as a man of blood, most likely because of the murder of Uriah. This illustrates, as in our modern society, if someone hires an assassin and the intended person is killed, God holds the instigator of the murder guilty of the murder. The one wielding the weapon is also guilty, but the major point here is the one who instigates the situation is also guilty of murder. God does not change (as stated several times in the Old Testament), so, if God's judgement in David's time frame is such, it is still the same today.

God is not double-minded, nor is He operating according to a double-standard, where if we do something it is sin, but if He does the same thing it is not sin for Him. The statement by God that we are to be holy as He is holy works both ways. Holiness is holiness no matter to whom it is applied. If God judged King David guilty of both adultery with Bathsheba, and murder by devising the scheme to have Uriah killed in battle, then if God devised the scheme whereby some are assigned to heaven and others to hell and the lake of fire, then God is the one guilty of the result of those spending eternity in the lake of fire. Obviously, God is not guilty of any sin, therefore, according to "Logical Consequence" above, the premise that God devised a scheme to assign some to heaven and others to hell, that premise is wrong. God did not devise a scheme which assigns some to heaven and others to hell. God does not control, nor predetermine our eternal destiny.

Luke 12:57 records Jesus saying to the crowd, " *Why do you not of your own initiative judge what is right?*" Those last four quoted words can be translated according to their basic definition as "make a decision for righteousness." God has created people with the initiative capable of making a decision for righteousness, otherwise, Jesus was lying to them and disqualified himself for being the blameless sacrifice for sins. John 1:12 tells us that "*...God gave people the "right to become children of God.*" The word "right" means:

"authority, power, right to govern, right to control." Putting that definition back into the phrase makes it read: ...God gave people "the authority, the power, the right to govern and control becoming children of God." People have the ability, authority, power to choose righteousness, or God, or becoming a child of God, and this is prior to salvation, according to what is actually written, what is actually inspired by God.

This "bad coin" has a flip side to it that is just as bad. In Ephesians 2:8 we are told that salvation is by grace through faith ("through" meaning: "by means of"). Romans 3:28 tells us that we are justified by faith. Faith is the key here. Abraham believed (had faith) in God and it was credited to him as righteousness (Rom. 4:3; Gal. 3:6; Gen. 15:6). Believing (having faith) is adverse to work according to Rom. 4:5. Faith is the most basic "hinge pin" of salvation. So, if God made the decision for who goes to heaven or hell, then there is no need for faith of any sort. If God made the decision, then our destiny is by fate, not by faith. We can either walk with God by sight or by faith, not by both.

In Job, we see in the first chapter that God set limits on Satan (don't touch Job's life), but did not define, nor suggest what Satan could do to see if Job would falter in his faith toward God. Satan chose to kill Job's seven children, destroy his fields and flocks, and afflict Job with boils. If God is in control as many people think, then God was controlling Satan to kill Job's children, thereby making God guilty of murder, as illustrated in the David-Nathan dialog above; Satan was simply God's murder weapon. Some think that we are not to violate God's moral law, but if God does, to Him it is not evil or sin. That ill-gotten belief goes against God and His word. If God controls us to do evil, sin, murder, coveting, etc., then by God's own word, God is guilty of those sins also.

We see the same type of thing in Judges chapter

11,where Jephthah winds up committing human sacrifice to God because of Jephthah's ill conceived "bargaining" with God to win a battle, and then "repay" God by sacrificing the first thing to walk out of his house when he returns from victory. It turned out to be Jephthah's daughter. If God controls us, then God is guilty of both Jephthah's ill-conceived vow and the human sacrifice to God which resulted. It should be obvious that God does not control people.

Other items.

Deut. 17:6, 19:15; Mat. 18:16; 2 Cor. 13:1; all indicate that conviction of an accusation requires two or three witnesses. Six witnesses have been presented indicating that God is not "in control" as most people understand "control."

Therefore, God does not "control" who goes to heaven or hell; who finds salvation or not. God does not "control" who gets blessings or rewards. God does not "control" our choice to sin in spite of our salvation. God does not control our "obedience" to his will (wish, desire, intent, with no concept of demand; i.e. what pleases Him). All these issues are to be a response based on our love for God, no control, power, force, or coercion of any sort is involved.

Proverbs 16:9 (NASB) "*⁹ The mind of man plans his way, But the Lord directs his steps.*"

Let's take a closer look at the word "directs."

(CWSB Dictionary) "*H3559.* כּוּן *kûn: A verb meaning to set up, to make firm, to establish, to prepare. The primary action of this verb is to cause to stand in an upright position, and thus the word also means fixed or steadfast. It signifies the action of setting in place or erecting an object (Isa. 40:20; Mic. 4:1); establishing a royal dynasty (2 Sam. 7:13; 1 Chr. 17:12); founding a city (Hab. 2:12); creating the natural order (Deut. 32:6; Ps. 8:3[4]; Prov. 8:27); fashioning a people for oneself (2 Sam. 7:24); adjusting weapons for targets (Ps. 7:12[13]; 11:2); appointing to an office (Josh. 4:4); confirming a position (1 Kgs. 2:12); making ready or preparing for use (2 Chr. 31:11; Ps. 103:19; Zeph. 1:7); attaining certainty (Deut. 13:14[15]; 1 Sam. 23:23).*"

(Vine's Complete Expository Dictionary) "*3559, "to be established, be readied, be prepared, be certain, be admissible."* "

The point of Prov. 16:9 is that God establishes and

makes firm, and prepares the steps that man's mind's plans require.

The meaning of the English verb "directs" in Prov. 16:9 means: "control the operations of; manage or govern" "Control" in this sense falls under Acts 10:38 where exercising control over a person (power to cause belief or behavior) is from the Devil. God does not contradict himself, nor does He "control" people. Therefore, the use of "directs" in Prov. 16:9 does not properly represent what the original language indicates – prepare or establish. These "plans" should obviously be according to His will (wish, desire, intent...).

Romans 1:24 (NASB) "*24 Therefore God gave them over in the lusts of their hearts to impurity, so that their bodies would be dishonored among them.*"

God does not change. This is iterated a few times in the bible.

Malachi 3:6 "*For I, the LORD, do not change; therefore you, O sons of Jacob, are not consumed.*", Numbers 23:19 , Psalm 102:25-27, Psalm 33:11, Isaiah 46:10 , Isaiah 43:10, Psalm 138:8 , Philippians 1:6 , Exodus 3:14 , Romans 11:29 , Titus 1:2 ,Hebrews 6:17 , James 1:17 , Hebrews 13:8 "*Jesus Christ is the same yesterday and today and forever.*"

God's way is to let people go the way of their heart's desire. Romans 1:24 describes one side of the situation: the evil are turned over to their evil desires. The other side of this situation is that the righteous are turned over to their righteous desires. (See 1 John 5:14-15) That is simply that those who want to please God because of their love for Him, are persuaded by the Holy Spirit to choose the righteous way (or righteous decision) in every situation. Those who choose sin and evil get the rewards of their sin and evil. Those who choose righteousness get the rewards of their choice in the situation – ultimately, an eternity in heaven in which righteousness dwells (2 Peter 3:13).

Romans 6:16 (NLT Study Bible) "*¹⁶ Don't you realize that you become the slave of whatever you choose to obey? You can be a slave to sin, which leads to death, or you can choose to obey God, which leads to righteous living.*"

Romans 6:16 (NASB) "*¹⁶ Do you not know that when you present yourselves to someone as slaves for obedience, you are slaves of the one whom you obey, either of sin resulting in death, or of obedience resulting in righteousness?*"

In Deuteronomy 28:1, Moses repeats what God said: "*If you listen to the voice of the Lord your God...,*" and then there are words of blessing. In Deuteronomy 28:15, Moses quotes God: "*If you do not listen to the voice of the Lord your God...,*" and many words of curses follow. There are more than three times as many words devoted to the curses as there are to the blessings. It is important to God that we listen to His voice. God does not change, Jesus is the same yesterday, today, and forever (see above). Jesus in John 10:27 tells us that His "*sheep hear his voice, and he knows them and they follow him.*" The word "follow" here means that we respond to God's voice on the basis of love, desiring to do those things which are pleasing to God. Both Old and New Testaments contain the principle that we need to listen to God's voice. "Believe," a verb, and "faith" a noun, are derivatives of the Greek word "persuade." Both words "believe" and "faith" mean "to have a firm persuasion." Persuasion comes to us through the still small voice of the Lord along with the message of the Gospel we speak to others. This is probably the most basic means of God interacting with people, by using His voice. The forces of nature and demons were commanded by God's voice in the Gospels. When it comes to people, those made in His image and likeness, God still uses His voice, but in the mode of persuasion, not force, coercion, irresistible pre-programimg, or anything else like that. Persuasion is an extreme opposite of a General giving orders to his troops. There are things which God commands us, like "do not fear," "repent," "turn the other cheek," and many other items that define for us what holy, godly behavior is that is pleasing to God. We have the option of not obeying those commands, and not doing things which are pleasing to God. The emphasis should be on doing those things pleasing to Him.

I have discussed this idea that "God is in control" with several people. I find it interesting that they become "unhinged," so to speak, as they respond to the very open-ended question: "Is God really in control?" In every case where I have asked that question, they come up with dozens of verse references that to them indicate God controls people the same way He controls demons and forces of nature. However, frequently mixed in with those references are statements to the effect that they need to have God in control. They use various ways and words to express that concept, but that phrase is the gist of what they are saying. Some have gone so far as to say that if God is not in control, then they cannot be saved. They seem to be incapable of realizing within those talks that they are superimposing a perceived need of the flesh onto Scripture to force it to mean that God is in control. That is technically called, "eisegesis." While exegesis is the process of drawing out the meaning from a text in accordance with the context and discoverable meaning of the words, eisegesis occurs when a reader imposes his or her interpretation or desired meaning into and onto the text.

God does not "control" the decisions and choices made by people. Most people treat "control" by God of their choices and actions as something that was preprogrammed, foreordained, and incontrovertibly set in eternal "stone," so to speak. People's choices determine the outcome of the situation, primarily regarding what goes on in their heart and mind, not necessarily any potential changes in the situation or it's context. God (the Holy Spirit) uses persuasion, not "control" or "power to cause," to guide the decisions of His children. God leaves us with free choice, both before and after salvation to choose following God's persuasion, or not following it. Martin Luther made a statement to the effect that he "could not abide a God who left to chance the choice by people for their salvation or damnation." This was Luther's opinion (eisegesis), he never referenced any Scripture to back up that statement. Unfortunately, Luther's opinion has had a tremendously detrimental influence on how people view God. After Luther's death, this became known as "chance is ungodly." (God ordained "chance" in Lev. 16:8, and works through chance in Prov. 16:33)

The point that many Christians miss is that our time here on Earth is our training (change) for eternity with God. The situations here on Earth are in a real sense totally irrelevant to eternity except for what they can be used for in changing us from fleshly minded and self-focused into heavenly and Godly minded for eternity. When God works all things together for good for those who love God and are called according to His purpose (Romans 8:28), the "good" being identified here is not our fleshly good, or anything remotely related to our fleshly existence, and usually not even related to the outcome of the situation. The "good" is focused on eternity, what is pleasing to God, not pleasing to our fleshly ideas or lusts; it is what satisfies His purpose, not ours. In Matthew 16:22-23, Jesus rebukes Peter for attempting to rebuke Jesus about His death and resurrection. The ending comment in verse 23 is Jesus telling Peter that Peter has his mind on things of men, not things of God. One of the issues in maturity is changing our focus from ourselves and our fleshly lusts and desires, toward God's purpose and God's goals, even if it results in our physical death.

Six Biblical Issues Against "God Is In Control"

Isa. 53:7-8 identifies Jesus being led away to death by oppression – Acts 10:38 identifies that oppression is from the devil. God is described as "love", "light with no darkness within", God does not sin, he does not tempt with evil, God does not commit evil or sin. (Heb. 2:18; James 1:13) So if God is in control, as many think, then God is the one doing the oppression to lead Jesus to death - He would have effectively murdered His own Son. Job identifies the "behind-the-scenes" activity in Job's life, Satan was the one executing the evil against Job within the limits God defined. God did not kill Job's children, nor destroy Job's fields and flocks. Satan did those things, not God. And without God "controlling" Satan in the process.

Parallelism within Isa. 53:7-8 – both use "oppression" or "oppressed", different words in Hebrew language – the oppression that was used to take Messiah to death is what is being emphasized – the action of the the devil. Parallelism in the Hebrew simply means that the same item or concept is repeated using different words, but the meaning is intended to be identical. This linguistic technique is used to emphasize a point.

God created mankind in his image and likeness. If we are truly "controlled" beings, and we are capable of creating things which "function" in certain ways, like computers, smartphones, electronic games, etc., but God must control everything about people, then I think we are missing a very serious point. Why can God not create people to function in certain ways, flip the switch on, and let people function the way God created them to function? If people create things with "functionality", then why could God not create people with "functionality"? God would still be "sovereign" over people if they function the way He created them. The typical concept of "God is in control" is based on the Dark Ages concept of control where people had to be constantly involved in getting things to act or behave certain ways. Theologians back then had no concept of advanced mechanics or automation, just like they had no sensibility related to Copernicus and Galileo determining the earth revolves around the sun. If you carefully study the theology of the Dark Ages, it becomes very apparent that theologians of that time used simplistic, human, fleshly limited concepts to understand the bible and limit God (the opposite of Paul's warning to the Colosians to distrust things based on fleshly or worldly concepts instead of trusting Christ, Col. 2:8-10). If we use their concept today, and we can create advanced automated mechanisms that function as created, then that makes us greater than the bible God of the Dark Ages. God is still greater than anything that can be created by people (e.g. DNA). 2 Peter 2 tells us that false teachers will arise from among the church.

It is all too easy for people to superimpose their own human limitations on God and His word, and never realize exactly what they are doing. God created mankind in order to fellowship with him, and that is what He did immediately after creating Adam and Eve, walking with them in the garden. (Gen. 3:8. Also, Rev. 4:11; Col. 1:16; Isa. 43:7; 1 Jn. 1:3; Jn. 15:15; ! Cor. 1:9) How much fellowship can a person have with their robot toy? Although the specific word "spontaneity" is not used in the Scriptures, I believe it is a good modern word to help us understand something of what holds relationships together. Something under control can never be spontaneous. A secular phrase that came about in the past few years may also help: "A random act of kindness." Suddenly you find yourself in a situation where the love of God in you can be expressed to another person, and you just do it. It would be very phony and unloving if those acts were always being controlled or preprogrammed. Real love between a husband and wife cannot exist if it is based on programmed response. If God controls us, then He controls what appears to us as "love" and that would make it completely phony; the same goes for what we see as our children's love for their parents.

If God could only create people who require constant control and manipulation so that anything can happen, and people can create advanced automated mechanical things that are capable of doing things on their own, then we are actually greater than God. Again, that is such a nonsensical conclusion, that the basic premise is wrong, that we people are created to be controlled.

God, not controlling our every quiver, gives us tremendous insight into God's personality and character, in whose image and likeness we are created. God made known His ways to Moses... (Psalm 103:7). Jesus was told by a man in the crowd, that "You teach God's ways." (Luke 12:21) Let God make known His ways and Himself to you...

How do things happen?

Matthew 4:4 (NASB) *"⁴ But He answered and said, "It is written, 'Man shall not live on bread alone, but on every word that proceeds out of the mouth of God.'"* "

One of the temptations that Satan presented to Jesus was to turn the stones into bread. Matthew 4:4 was Jesus' response. We are to live by every word that comes from the mouth of God. 2 Timothy 3:16 tells us that Scripture is inspired by God, or "God-breathed." The Holy Spirit spoke the words of Scripture to the many "scribes" who recorded them. 2 Corinthians 2:13 tells us that Paul spoke words of God to the Corinthians, not just the words, but how to express them (the last word in that verse in the Greek means "to express"). The words that are recorded for us are the words we need to live by. Many religious philosophies practice deception by claiming that what is actually written does not really mean what it says, but there is something else, part of their philosophy, that carries the "true" meaning. If that were to be the correct way to read God's word, then they are also claiming that what is actually written is wrong, essentially a lie, which is opposite of what Scripture actually tells us. That is the very same thing the serpent did to Eve in Genesis 3, which brought sin into humanity. We must be careful to read what is actually there and not modify it, even if we do not initially understand it. God has a curse on modifying his word, which some groups openly ignore – see Deut. 4:2, 18:18-20; Prov. 30:6; Jer. 26:2; Rev. 22:18-19. We are instructed by God to pay attention to all of his words and not add to them or omit (leave out) any of his words.

That brings us to what the real question should be: "If God is not in control, then why and how do things happen or take place? But before we answer that question, we need to define some more terms. Let's review Acts10:38 again from

34

Six Biblical Issues Against "God Is In Control"

Issue 1. The statement is made about Jesus that he *"went about doing good, healing and delivering those who were oppressed by the devil"*. This very obviously tells us that oppression comes from the devil. In the Greek, the word oppressed means "to exercise power over another." The word control means: "the power to influence or direct people's behavior or the course of events:" This is the same basic meaning as what the Greek states for the word oppressed; even though the specific words used in the definitions of the two words are slightly different, the obvious meaning of both words is identical. So we see that control and oppression are the same thing. It should not take very much to identify the fact that "control," the way most people think about it, comes from the devil in regards to people.

In John 1:12, God gives people the right to become children of God. The word "right" means: "authority, power, right to govern and control." This verse tells us that God gave people the authority, power, right to govern and control becoming a child of God. Both the Holy Spirit and the devil start off on the same level playing field of persuasion. Repentance is a change of mind,and when the Holy Spirit persuades us of sin righteousness and judgment, as the Apostle John stated in John 16:8, this very simply identifies to us that we are sinners, Jesus is the righteous one who can save us, and we need to make a decision. (The word judgment here in the Greek simply means to "decide, make a decision".) There are many places in the Bible where God tells us that he does not change. Another way of stating that is, God is consistent. So if we start off in salvation by making a decision, then it should be obvious that we continue our relationship with God, by continuing to make decisions.

In 1 Corinthians 1:18, we are told that we are being saved, it should be an on-going process from spiritual infancy to spiritual maturity. Our continued relationship with God should be a series of continued decisions for holiness and righteousness. The Holy Spirit continues to persuade us after our initial salvation, but now to encourage us to choose righteousness in each situation. Over the years, I have heard many Christians say that they missed God's leading and therefore failed to find a blessing that they would have had if they had followed the leading of the Spirit. In every situation we encounter, there needs to be a decision and this is how things happen, how things take place. God does not change, so if he is consistent, and since he gave us the authority, the power, the right to govern and control becoming children of God, and as we progress in faith, the decisions we make for righteousness are key to how and why things happen. When we make a decision (one way or the other) and follow through on it, then things happen, or don't happen.

If you think about it carefully, you should realize that Satan does not want us to understand all of this so that we do not make the choices and decisions for righteousness that we should be making. In some situations, the Jonah principal kicks in. Jonah did not want to preach to the people of Nineveh. They were enemies of the Jews, and if they turned to God, they would not be punished for the sins that they had already committed against the Jews. Jonah did not want them to go unpunished. In many ways Christians today can behave just like Jonah. They secretly, and frequently only subconsciously, want someone to be punished for the bad or evil things they have done. So, we fail to make the decision for righteousness, we fail to present God's word to them in hopes that they get punished. At the judgment seat of Christ, I do not want to be asked any questions about why I did not choose righteousness in a situation like that, and not help provide someone with a means of finding salvation and forgiveness, that is the same as being unforgiving... (which is another unforgivable sin).

Many times we say that God is in control so that we do not have to make these kinds of choices. "If it doesn't work out, it just was not God's will, (frequently meaning that God did not command or control it that way)." When in reality, we have failed to choose righteousness and therefore what happens is evil instead of a blessing.

When other Christians are involved, we should make the choice for righteousness. If we simply remain silent, we will not be opening the way for a blessing to that other Christian, or a blessing for ourselves either. When unbelievers are involved, a choice for silence, or not choosing righteousness, can be their eternal death knell. It's not just the tongue that has the power of death and life... it can involve the decisions behind the use, or non-use, of the tongue.

2 Peter 3:11-12 (NASB) "*11...what sort of people ought you to be in holy conduct and godliness, 12 looking for and hastening the coming of the day of God,...*"

The word "hastening" in this verse from 2 Peter means "to urge on." This is written within the context of the end times final judgments, including the "plagues" in Rev. 11 (two witnesses), the punishments brought against the Antichrist's world system, the cleansing of the earth from the effects of sin and evil brought about by Satan and human sin. We complain that it is taking God so long to send Jesus back to rapture the prepared believers, but we insist that we do nothing to bring that about. We abdicate our responsibility (we fail to make the correct "response") and wonder what is taking so long.

Luke 12:57 (NASB) "*57 "And why do you not even on your own initiative judge what is right?"*"

The word for "judge" simply means "to decide, make a decision." The word "right" is also translated in other places as "righteousness." Here, Jesus is stating to those not yet born again, that it is of our own initiative to make the decision for righteousness. We have the God created ability to choose righteousness. It is our own, not provided to us at the moment of need. Otherwise, Jesus is lying to us, deceiving us into thinking there is something about us when there really is not.

James 2:17 (ESV) "*17 So also faith by itself, if it does not have works, is dead.*"

This verse in James very clearly identifies that our salvation is to produce "works." This simply means the things we say, do, our expressed (and mental) attitudes toward a situation, i.e., our behavior in each and every situation. This is what I mean by "follow through on" above. When we make a decision it needs to be expressed in action or behavior of some form. Otherwise our alleged "faith" is dead. This is not "works" to earn salvation – these "works" are the visible evidence that salvation exists within the person performing the "works."

The evening of Christ's resurrection the disciples were sealed with the Holy Spirit for salvation. The Greek behind "Receive the Holy Spirit" means that right there, right then they received the Holy Spirit and the Holy Spirit continued with them (imperative, present-continuing). Forty days later, Jesus ascended to heaven, and just before that he told the disciples to wait in the city until they were clothed with power from on high (Luke 24:49 & Acts 1:4-5). The disciples had two encounters with the Holy Spirit. The second encounter was for the power to carry out the spreading of the Gospel and persevere under persecution, it was not to be done in the strength of the flesh, but the power of the Holy Spirit. The baptism with the Holy Spirit gives us the power to understand what is the choice for righteousness in any situation and the power to follow through on that decision.

Matthew 12:36-37 (NASB) "*36 But I tell you that every careless word that people speak, they shall give an account-*

ing for it in the day of judgment. [37] For by your words you will be justified, and by your words you will be condemned."

Proverbs 18:21 (NASB) *"[21] Death and life are in the power of the tongue,..."*

Think about the possibility of what could happen if we stopped tossing the choice back "to God" and started exercising his created ability in us to make the choices ourselves and then follow through on those choices? Our judgment (rewards or lack of) will be based on our words, not on Satan's lie that God decided before the foundation of the world. If we believe that God has raised Jesus from death and confess Him with our mouth, we shall be saved. Our belief, our words, our behavior, all work together for either good or evil. It is our choice, through our actions and words that make things happen. Throwing everything to "God is in control" simply abdicates our responsibility to choose righteousness, and by default chooses evil.

Six Biblical Issues Against "God Is In Control"

40

Six Biblical Issues Against "God Is In Control"

*9 7 8 0 9 8 5 3 4 6 0 8 9 *